FATHER BROWNE'S
ENGLAND

Father Browne with Field-Marshal Earl Alexander of Tunis when the latter was Minister for Defence (1953).

FATHER BROWNE'S
ENGLAND

FATHER BROWNE'S
ENGLAND

E. E. O'DONNELL SJ

WOLFHOUND PRESS

First Published in 1996 by
WOLFHOUND PRESS
68 Mountjoy Square
Dublin 1

ISBN 0 86327 490 0

British Library Cataloguing in Publication data: a catalogue record for this book
is available from the British Library.

Profits made by the Jesuit Order from the sale of Father Browne's books
and prints go to the Jesuit Solidarity Fund established to help counteract Ireland's
serious unemployment problems both north and south of the Border.

Book and cover design: Ted & Ursula O'Brien, Oben Design, Dublin.
Photographic prints by Davison & Associates, Dublin.
Duotone separations by Colour Repro Ltd, Dublin.
Typeset by Oben Design.
Printed in Hong Kong through World Print Ltd.

Cover photographs:
Front: *On the River Waveney, East Anglia (1935).*
Back: *Delivering the milk at Lavenham (1933).*

CONTENTS

INTRODUCTION

IN 1985 I was working as an assistant to the Jesuit Provincial Superior in Dublin. My duties included the retrieval from the archives in the basement of old documents whenever legal or historical matters required documentation. In the archives there was an old trunk, buried beneath a hundredweight of papers and files. I had often wondered what was in it.

One day, when I was less busy than usual, I decided to unearth this evidently much-travelled trunk. When I had cleared away the overlying documents I was able to read the chalked words written on its lid. They read: "Father Browne's Photographs". Intrigued, I opened the trunk and discovered that it was full of packs of negatives, all neatly captioned and dated. "Aboard the Titanic, April 1912", "Irish Guards at Watch on the Rhine, January 1919", "Australia v England: Test Match Cricket, Adelaide, February 1925", "Rev. Ronald Knox preaching at Walsingham, May 1935": these were among the 42,000 captions that emerged. And the photographs were excellent. It was a veritable treasure trove.

I was soon put in touch with the Head of the Department of Photography in Dublin's Kevin Street College of Technology. A member of the Irish Professional Conservators and Restorers Association, David Davison was spellbound by what he saw but had to give me the bad news that the photographs were on nitrate-based film that was rapidly deteriorating. The whole collection would have to be transferred to safety film —

a costly operation that would have to be carried out without further ado. To its great credit, Allied Irish Bank agreed to finance the work.

FATHER BROWNE

Francis Mary Hegarty Browne was born in Cork in 1880, and began taking photographs at the age of seventeen when he toured Europe with his brother and his Kodak camera. On returning to Ireland he joined the Jesuit Order and, after two years of noviceship near Tullamore, attended the Royal University in Dublin where he was a classmate of James Joyce. The budding author knew Frank Browne well and featured him as "Mr Browne the Jesuit" in *Finnegans Wake*. Unfortunately the photographer-to-be was not allowed to own a camera at this stage of his studies, so we have no Browne portrait of the writer as a young man.

Three years studying philosophy at Chieri, near Turin in Italy (1902–1905) were formative ones for Frank Browne because during the summer months he made a serious study of Italian paintings in the galleries of Genoa, Milan, Florence and Venice. He learned a lot about the perspective, balance and composition of pictures that would stand to him later in his own photographic work.

From 1906 to 1911 Frank was a teacher at Belvedere College in Dublin where both Joyce and he had been to school. In 1906 he founded the Camera Club that is still thriving — and that gave him a good reason for having a camera of his own. Eventually he would own two Zeiss cameras and a Leica. He published articles on photography in *The Belvederian*, the college annual which he founded in 1906 and continued to edit until 1911.

Aboard the *Titanic*

The final stage of his studies, four years of theology, took place at Milltown Park, Dublin. During his second year there his Uncle Robert, Bishop of Cloyne, bought him a ticket for the first two legs of the maiden voyage of the *Titanic*. His first extant English photographs, therefore, were taken in April 1912 at Waterloo Station, London. Sailing from Southampton to Cherbourg and thence to Queenstown (now Cobh) in County Cork, Frank took many memorable pictures aboard the doomed liner, including the last extant photograph of

Front page of London's Daily Sketch, *18 April, 1912.*

Captain Edward Smith and the only photograph ever taken in the Marconi-room of the *Titanic*. After the disaster, Frank Browne's pictures appeared on the front pages of newspapers around the world.

Ordained for War

On 31st July, 1915, Frank was ordained a priest. Shortly afterwards he was assigned as Chaplain to the Irish Guards whom he served for four years on the front lines in France and Flanders. He lived through the horrors of the Somme, Ypres and Passchendaele, being injured five times and gassed once. He recovered from his wounds at Warley Barracks in Essex and at Wellington Barracks, London. Described by his commanding officer Colonel (later Field-Marshal) Alexander as "the bravest man I ever met", Father Browne won the M.C. and Bar and the *Croix de Guerre*. In the Irish Guards Association Journal, Lord Nugent wrote: "Everyone in the Battalion, officer or man, Catholic or Protestant, loved and respected Father Browne and he had great influence for good."

After World War I, Father Browne remained with the Irish Guards in Germany. A treasured possession of those guards at their headquarters in Wellington Barracks, London, is a beautifully-bound Browne album of photographs entitled 'The Watch on the Rhine'.

Australian Interlude

Back in Ireland in 1920, Father Browne became Superior of the Church of St Francis Xavier, Gardiner Street, Dublin. Here his health deteriorated. He developed serious lung trouble due to the wartime mustard-gassing and his doctor prescribed a sea voyage and a warmer climate. Thus he spent the two years, 1924 and 1925, in Australia. His photographs of that continent appeared in book form last year. They show Sydney without its Harbour Bridge — let alone its Opera House — Melbourne, Brisbane, Adelaide, Perth and Fremantle, as well as many outback areas which he pictured in all their pastoral splendour.

His voyage to Australia was by way of South Africa;

The first and last Titanic *Special at Waterloo Station, London. Mr Astor on the left. Father Browne took this train to Southampton on the morning of 10th April, 1912.*

on the return journey he visited Ceylon (now Sri Lanka), the Cocos Island, Aden, Suez, Salonika, Naples, Toulon, Gibraltar, Algeciras and Lisbon — thus adding an important international dimension to his photographic collection.

Photographic Salon

On returning to Ireland, Father Browne resumed his work at Gardiner Street Church and in 1929 was appointed to the Retreats and Missions staff of the Irish Jesuits. This assignment, which would last for the rest of his life, brought him to thousands of parishes throughout the four 'Home Countries'. Since his preaching was mainly done in the evenings, he had the daylight hours to pursue his photographic work.

In 1927 he became a Vice President of the first Irish International Salon of Photography, under the presidency of Sir John Lavery RA. This venture was so successful that it was repeated every second year up to the outbreak of World War II. Father Browne exhibited his own work at these exhibitions and won several prizes.

The inspiration for this Salon came from a friend of Father Browne, George Davison, Managing Director of the Kodak Company at Harrow. Davison was a prominent photographer in his own right. He had been a founder of the secessionist movement called 'The Linked Ring' in 1892. This group founded the London Salon of Photography and eventually recombined with the Royal Photographic Society in 1910. Obviously Father Browne had found a kindred spirit in George Davison who, in return for monthly articles in *The Kodak Magazine*, gave the Irish priest a free supply of film for life.

England

In 1930 Father Browne's home base was changed from Dublin to Emo Court in County Laois, the home of Lord Portarlington, which had just been converted into a Jesuit novitiate. Besides his work in Ireland, his duties included the preaching of parish 'missions' in England and the directing of retreats for nuns in places like York, Northampton and Beaconsfield. In those days a Parish Mission lasted for a fortnight: a week for the women and a week for the men. We know that he was very good at this work: frequently he was asked back. He did much photographic work for the Church of England, and Roman Catholic pilgrimages to Walsingham and Dunwich were photographed in detail. The preachers there included people like Cardinal Bourne, Vernon Johnston SJ, Fabian Dix OP, Ronald Knox and Martin D'Arcy SJ.

He also had many family connections with England. His eldest brother, James, was an eye specialist at London's Southwark Hospital and lived in Bromley, Kent. He had a nephew, Robert, living in Weston-super-Mare. His sister, Margaret, was married to Dr Robert Martin whose practice was at Rodney Street in Liverpool.

While in London, Father Browne often stayed with his friend Lord Alexander and with the Jesuits at Farm Street Church. Elsewhere in England, when he was not residing with the local clergy, he stayed with Lady Ashburnham near Norwich and with the Booth family of Lewes, Sussex.

Overall, he took over three thousand photographs of England and many more in Scotland and Wales.

Father Browne died in 1960. Lord Alexander visited him on his deathbed and attended his funeral at Glasnevin Cemetery in Dublin. Since he had taken 42,000 photographs by the time of his death, it is not surprising to discover that one of them is of the Jesuit burial-plot where he now rests in peace.

Post-Mortem

For twenty-five years following his death, the treasure trove which I chanced upon in 1985 lay unnoticed in the Jesuit archives. And to my added astonishment at what the Features Editor of *The Sunday Times* then described as "the photographic equivalent of the discovery of the Dead Sea Scrolls", I noted that the thousands of negatives were all neatly captioned and dated. Such meticulous recording of his negatives suggests the photographer's own awareness of the historical significance of his work as social documentation of his time and also undoubtedly as his contribution to the art of photography.

In my biography *Father Browne: A Life in Pictures*, David Davison gave a professional assessment of the work of Father Browne:

"My initial excitement for Father Browne's photography was so intense that during the following weeks I found myself wondering whether I might have over-reacted and that perhaps a more sober assessment was required. This reappraisal has continued for some years now during which time my son Edwin and I have made new negatives of the entire collection and created a computerised database. This enhanced familiarity with the Collection has in fact confirmed my initial appraisal of the significance of his work. There is no other Collection of twentieth-century Irish photography of such stature, none so large, so wide in range of subject or rival in terms of artistic achievement. Father Browne's work is not just of significance for Ireland: I believe that as it becomes more widely known he will be acknowledged as one of the great photographers of the first half of this century.

"His writings indicate his consciousness of the artistic potential of photography and he took vigorous steps to promote the medium, particularly in the establishment of the Irish Salon. His friendship with George Davison was no doubt significant in this context. Davison's commitment to photography as a means of artistic expression is well documented. No doubt he encouraged Father Browne in this regard in addition to the provision of free film.

"…The Collection contains most of his life's production, including many casual group pictures of friends and of the many priests and nuns he met whilst conducting missions and performing other preaching duties. Included are those pictures that did not quite work. Sometimes due to lack of suitable film, sometimes as a result of being over ambitious. It is unusual to have so complete a set of negatives because many photographers have enhanced their reputations by removing all evidence of their failures. An outstanding feature of Father Browne's work is that there are thousands of really fine images, always captioned, whilst the remaining negatives give a fascinating insight into his photographic persona."

Publications and Exhibitions

Shortly after my discovery of the negatives, Wolfhound Press in Dublin included over one hundred Browne photographs in my *Annals of Dublin* (1987). Since then, five further volumes of Browne photographs have been published by Wolfhound — *Father Browne's Ireland, The Genius of Father Browne, Father Browne's Dublin, Father Browne's Cork* and *Father Browne's Australia.* To mark its silver jubilee, The Society of Irish Foresters published *Father Browne's Woodland Images,* and in the French language *L'Irlande du père Browne* was published earlier this year by Anatolia Editions, Paris.

Allied Irish Bank used Father Browne photographs for its mass-circulation calendar in 1992. Then Ark Life Assurance (AIB's subsidiary company) began showing magnificent Father Browne exhibitions which have now been seen in over sixty locations around Ireland.

A small exhibition of prints has already been shown by AIB-Britain at its Uxbridge Bankcentre and at some of its English branches. The bank is currently planning a major exhibition that will tour the world.

The Guinness Hop Store held an exhibition of the Dublin photographs which attracted record crowds. Then RTÉ, Ireland's national television network, commissioned a series of six television programmes entitled 'The Day Before Yesterday' and based entirely on Father Browne's work. Most recently, the Georges Pompidou Centre in Paris has mounted a Browne exhibition which was seen by 20,000 people daily for two months before moving to the Cultural Centre at Montpellier in the south of France.

Prints

Profits made by the Jesuit Order from the sale of Browne books and prints (the latter are available from Davison & Associates, Dublin) go to the Jesuit Solidarity Fund which was set up to help counteract Ireland's serious unemployment problem, both north and south of the Border. The building of an inter-denominational community centre in Portadown is an example of the kind of project which the new Fund finances.

Father Browne, who did so much charitable work during his lifetime and who established what he quaintly called "Brownie Burses" to fund his charities, will be glad to know in his heavenly abode that the good he did was not interred with his bones.

The Capital

The photographer was a frequent visitor to London and was always a welcome guest of the Irish Guards at Wellington Barracks. Many of his pictures, therefore, were taken around Birdcage Walk and its environs. More frequent than his considered views of public buildings (such as the Palace of Westminster and Tower Bridge) are his candid shots of the city in action. The photographs taken through the windscreens of taxis, for example, show ordinary things at extraordinary angles with memorable results.

Motorized traffic gives way to horse-drawn transport on High Holborn (1936).

Right:
St Clement Danes, one of London's many churches designed by Christopher Wren (1936). Situated on an island in the middle of The Strand, it was badly damaged by bombs on 10th May, 1941.

Below:
Waiting for the bus, outside Victoria Station (1936). A double-decker bus with open-air staircase can be seen approaching.

Facing page:
Fleet Street (1935) when it was the hub of the newspaper-publishing business. Note the rolls of newsprint on the lorry opposite the offices of The Morning Post.

*Facing page:
Pointsman
conducting the
traffic on Kingsway
(1936).*

*'Ask a Policeman',
New Oxford Street
(1936).*

Facing page, above:
Liverpool Street Station (1933). The Great Eastern Hotel can be seen in the background. Father Browne often used this terminus en route to East Anglia.

Facing page, below:
Morning riders near Hyde Park Corner (1936). Taken through the windscreen of a taxi-cab; the horsemen are heading for the bridle path in Green Park.

Right:
Queen Victoria Monument, seen through the gates of Buckingham Palace (1936).

Below:
Playing 'Pooh-sticks'? Something has caught the children's attention on the bridge in St James's Park (1936).

Right:
Westminster Bridge, Big Ben and
the Houses of Parliament (1930).

Below:
Tower Bridge admits the passage of
a steamer (1936).

Left:
The empty pedestal outside the National Gallery (1928) prompts Father Browne's question: "To the unknown God?"

Below:
The Victoria Embankment with dual-carriage tramway (1932). Cleopatra's Needle can be seen on the left.

Seeking and finding directions, Trafalgar Square (1936). The church in the background is St Martin-in-the-Fields.

Urban Life

With the exception of the industrial municipalities of the Midlands, Father Browne photographed most of the towns and cities of England, spanning the country from Chester to Great Yarmouth, from Durham to Southampton. He did not focus on the major buildings, although sometimes (as in the Liverpool picture shown here) these can be seen in the background. His photographs often show bill-boards or shop signs that capture something of the essence of England, its traditions, its enduring values.

Lindum Road, Lincoln (1934). Taken from the top of Broadgate, the photograph shows the cathedral on the sky-line.

Right:
Bridewell Alley, Norwich (1933) is overlooked by the tower of St Andrew's Church.

Below:
Great Yarmouth, showing St Mary's Jesuit Church (1931).

Facing page:
The River Cherwell as it flows past Magdalen College, Oxford (1936). The Botanic Gardens are in the foreground.

Left:
Winchester (1936), showing 'Ye Olde Hostel of God Begot'.

Below:
Aboard a Mersey ferry-boat with Liverpool in the background (1939).

Facing page:
Browsing at the bookshop, Oxford (1936). The Conference on Academic Freedom is to be addressed by Bertrand Russell.

Facing page:
'The Plain' or Market
Place of Great
Yarmouth
(1931) with the Church
of St Nicholas in the
background.

Right:
At the entrance to
The Shambles, York
(1926).

The Weavers at Canterbury (1919). The River Stour still flows beneath the windows of these old houses which stand on a small island.

On one of 'The Rows' of Great Yarmouth (1933). These narrow lanes lead inland from the Marine Parade and still bustle with activity each summer.

The High Bridge (12th Century) over the River Witham in Lincoln (1934). Its half-timbered houses were built in 1540.

Below:
The Bar Convent, York, seen through Micklegate (1926).

Right: High Street, Cromer (1933).

Below left:
The first Belisha Beacons in Bristol, near the Fishponds (1949). The church in the background is St Joseph's.

Below right:
The Market Hall at Abingdon (1936).

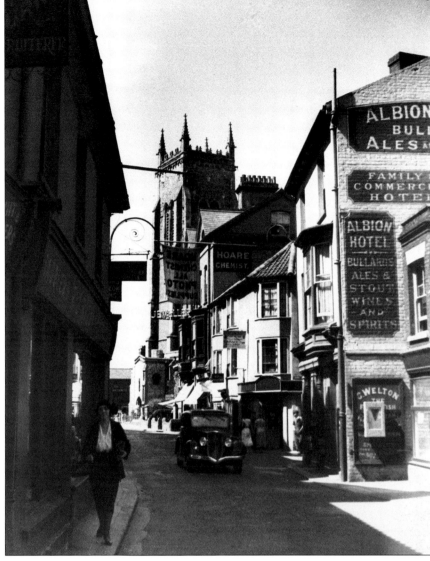

Facing page:
Winchester (1936), taken from the steps of the Guildhall.

Right:
Micklegate, York (1926). The unsightly electric tram-wires are things of the past.

Below:
The Municipal Buildings, York, from Lendal Bridge (1926).

Illegal entry! Birkenhead (1939).

Cathedrals

During the 1930s, the Kodak Company of Harrow-on-the-Hill commissioned Father Browne to photograph the great cathedrals of England and published his features on them in *The Kodak Magazine*. Besides photographing the magnificent Church of England buildings in detail, the priest also visited the newer Roman Catholic cathedrals, including the one in Liverpool which was still at an early stage of construction. His exterior views often included an extraneous item that gave them a personal touch.

The moat surrounding the Bishop's Palace at Wells (1949). The towers of the Cathedral can be seen behind the trees.

Westminster Cathedral from the corner of Ashley Place (1936). The church in the foreground, St Andrew's, was destroyed during the Blitz.

An unusual view of the towers and magnificent West Front of York Minster, taken from Duncombe Place (1926).

Left:
Ely Cathedral: the 'lantern' from College Park (1934).

Above:
Interior of 'lantern', Ely Cathedral (1934).

Facing page:
The towers of Lincoln Cathedral from the west (1934).

Right:
The Norman crypt of Canterbury Cathedral, completed in 1107, is said to be the finest in England (1919).

Below:
St John's Roman Catholic Cathedral, Northampton, is tucked away off Bridge Street (1949).

Facing page:
The Nave of Winchester Cathedral (1936), taken for The Kodak Magazine.

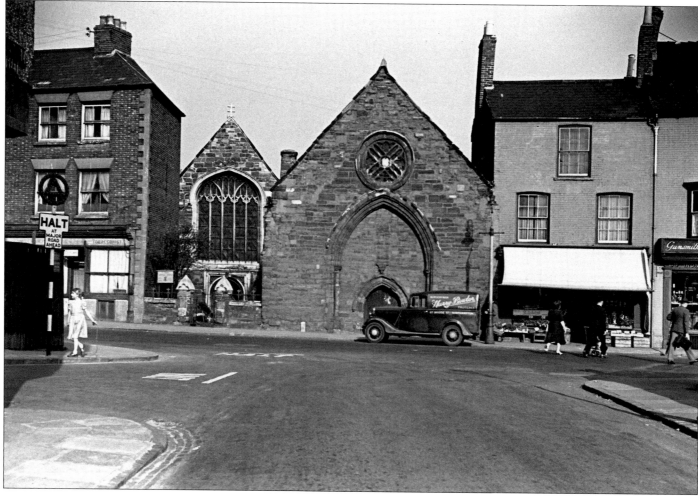

Bath Abbey (1949) overlooking the Roman Baths. The Abbey replaced Wells as the cathedral of Somerset from 1090 to 1218.

Among Father Browne's photographs of English cathedrals was a series of photographs of paintings of Durham Cathedral, taken in 1919. This is one of these and it shows how, during his early years in Italy, he had learned much about photography from the study of classical paintings.

Durham Cathedral, a masterpiece of Romanesque architecture, was begun in 1093 and completed, except for the towers, in less than forty years.

Above left:
The attenuated cloisters of Christchurch Cathedral, Oxford
(1935), which were destroyed during the Civil War.

Above:
Westminster Abbey (1930). This served as London's cathedral
in the sixteenth century. A view of St Paul's Cathedral appears
in a later chapter.

Left:
Construction of Roman Catholic cathedral at Liverpool,
showing the completion of an archway into the crypt (1935).

Facing page:
Norwich Cathedral, the West Front (1931).

The medieval clock at Wells (1949). On the left is one of the famous 'scissors' arches, constructed to support the tower of the cathedral in 1338.

Architecture

During the 1930s, Father Browne was commissioned by the Church of England's Council for the Care of Churches to photograph its buildings in East Anglia and the treasures which they contained. In this chapter we see some of the buildings he photographed; in the next chapter we see several of their treasures. Even before this task began, the photographer was already doing this kind of work at places like South Weald and Shenfield in Essex and at West Wickham in Surrey.

The interior of Greenstead Hall, near Halstead, Essex (1919).

Right:
Stonyhurst College, Lancashire (1926), with Fr W. Weld SJ at the reflecting pool. Former pupil Arthur Conan Doyle used this building as a model for 'Baskerville Hall'.

Below:
The Observatory at Stonyhurst College (1926). First-year pupils here, as in other Jesuit schools, belonged to a class called 'Elements': hence Sherlock Holmes' "Elementary!"

Facing page:
Mossley Hill Convent, near Manchester (1947). The French Château style of architecture is unusual in this area.

The High Altar of the chapel at Ampleforth College, Yorkshire (1926). The modern Benedictine abbey here rivals its predecessors of bygone centuries.

The parish church at South Weald, Essex (1919). The climbing plants and rose-beds, in Father Browne's view, added to its attractions.

Right:
The shrine of St Edmund at Bury St Edmunds (1930).
The wall of the ancient monastic enclosure can be seen
on the right.

Facing page:
West Wickham Church, Surrey (1931), from the east.
The church has some fine 15th-century stained-glass
windows.

Left:
Shenfield Church, Essex (1919), with its graceful
14th-century spire of oak.

Below:
West View, Ratcliffe College, Leicester (1930). This picture
is included as an example of how, quite frequently, Father
Browne's photographs were turned into postcards.

West View,
Ratcliffe College, Leicester.

Right:
The Angel Roof of the church at Knapton, Norfolk (1933). The medieval roof has supporting beams with 'modern' angels as corbels.

Below:
The ancient round tower of the church at Little Snoring, Norfolk (1933). Its tiled roof and weather-vane are fairly recent additions.

Antiquities

Besides working for the Church of England, Father Browne was also commissioned by the British Museum to photograph certain antiquities of East Anglia. He worked for Thomas Downing Kendrick who was Keeper of the Department of British and Medieval Antiquities and who went on to become Director of the museum from 1950 to 1959. Although the photographer covered such well-known sites as Castle Acre and Walsingham Abbey, he also focused on the less famous treasures shown here.

'Unusual Tombstone' at Gillingham, Norfolk (1933), marks the grave of a deep-sea diver.

Quaint wording on an eighteenth-century tombstone in Winchester (1935).

Above left:
Carved bench-ends at Blythburgh Church, Suffolk (1931).
This carving represents 'The Fervent One'; others have such names
as 'The Apostle' and 'The Publican'.

Above right:
Wooden effigies on the tomb of Sir Michael de la Pole and his wife,
Kathleen, at Wingfield Church, Suffolk (1933). Sir Michael was
killed at Harfleur in 1415. These carvings are said to be "the best
of their date". (Published by courtesy of the Trustees of the British Museum.)

Left:
Stained-glass window at Martham, Norfolk (1931). The central
figure represents Saint Michael.

Left:
Detail of carving on the wooden Town Hall on Lady Street, Lavenham, Suffolk (1933). Of all the places that Father Browne photographed, Lavenham is the least changed, the best preserved.

Above, centre:
Old Norman door at Haddiscoe Church, Norfolk (1930). The reinforcing wrought ironwork is unusually ornamental.

Above, right:
The 15th-century Font of the Four Evangelists at Haddiscoe Church, Norfolk (1930).

Right: The thatched Church of All Saints and Saint Margaret, Pakefield, Suffolk (1930), has a porch with mounted sun-dial.

Far right: The High Street at Wymondham, Norfolk (1935). The Tudor-style houses and Market Cross with timbered upper storey are among the oldest in the country.

Facing page: The carved lych-gate at Barsham Church, Suffolk (1931). The thatching on the gate matches the roof of the church.

The Market Cross at North Walsham, Norfolk (1933) stands beneath the Market Clock. With bicycles and 'Baby' Austins.

Rural England

Since Father Browne put captions and dates on all his negatives, rarely making prints of them, it is evident that he had an eye to the future. He must have been certain that, in years to come, the rural England he was photographing would be changed beyond recognition. This is especially clear in his pictures of farming methods and of agricultural machinery. The horses seen in this chapter are already giving way to the tractor shown near Gillingham.

A ramble through the village of Sparham, Norfolk (1934).

Below:
*'The Triple Plea' inn at Halesworth, Suffolk
(1933) with Anthony Walsh standing to attention.*

Right:
Close-up of 'The Triple Plea' inn-board.

Facing page:
*Ancient lamp-arch and Priory House, Blythburgh,
Suffolk (1930).*

Right:
In the harvest field near Gillingham,
Norfolk (1931).

Below:
Watering the horses near Whissonsett,
Norfolk (1934).

Facing page:
Harvest time at Aldeby, Norfolk (1933).

Right:
Climbers reach the summit of Scafell Pike (1928). At 3,162 feet, this is the highest point in England. It overlooks Wast Water in the Lake District.

Below:
Self-portrait of Father Browne at the head of Piers Fell, facing the Great Gable, Cumbria (1928). His camera must have had a lengthy time-release for this picture to be possible.

Left:
Wayside rest after
exploring Hadrian's Wall
near Hexham,
Northumberland (1935).

Below:
The Hastings family
enjoys a picnic at
Shooter's Hill near
Gillingham, Norfolk
(1931).

Facing page:
A big turn-out for the Tennis Finals at Bungay, Suffolk,
on 5th September, 1931.

Right:
Pastoral scene near Dorchester, Dorset (1930).

Below:
Playing croquet at the Throckmortons' house,
Beccles, Suffolk (1933).

'Firelight Stories':
Mrs Hastings reads to
her sons, Francis and
Michael, at
Gillingham, Norfolk
(1931).

Mrs Taylor in the garden of 'Heatherbrae' near Castle Rising, Norfolk (1935).

Right:
Mrs Kenyon of Gillingham, Norfolk (1933).

Below:
Mrs Booth minds the horses, Lewes, Sussex (1935).

Lady Gurney (on right) bids farewell to the Cowan family at Walsingham, Norfolk (1936).

Right:
Most Rev. Leo Parker, Bishop of Northampton, with Canon Ruddenham. Taken after a Confirmation ceremony at Northampton (1949).

Below:
Fr Martin D'Arcy SJ preaching to the crowds assembled for the Dunwich Pilgrimage, Suffolk (1936).

Fr Ronald Knox preaching in the rain at the shrine of the Blessed Virgin,
Walsingham, Norfolk (1935).

Right:
Ursula Martin with her Afghan hound on the Sussex Downs near Lewes (1935).

Below:
Junior Girls starting line-up at Gillingham Sports, Norfolk (1931).

Right:
John Trafford becomes a mechanic! Taken at Dunborough, Norfolk (1935).

Below:
John Taylor fixes his electric train at Fritton Decoy, Norfolk (1936).

82

*Lady Catherine
Ashburnham
greeting students
from Upholland
College at
Walsingham
(1935).
The students had
walked all the
way from
Liverpool to
Norfolk on
pilgrimage to the
Slipper Chapel,
seen here in the
background.*

Apprentice D. Greene being seen off by his mother and sister on his first voyage aboard the SS Port of Melbourne, *Falmouth, Cornwall (1924).*

Mr T.W. Norman delivering the milk at Lavenham, Suffolk (1933).

Irish Guards

Immediately after his ordination to the priesthood in 1915, Frank Browne was assigned as Chaplain to the Irish Guards. Most of his army photographs were taken in France, Belgium and Germany and so do not qualify for inclusion in this book. In 1919, the Chaplain divided his time between the forces left on the Rhine and those who had returned to England. The latter are shown here, mostly at Warley Barracks in Essex and at their headquarters at Wellington Barracks, London.

'Quick March!' The band of the Irish Guards leads the parade from Wellington Barracks to Buckingham Palace (1919).

Right:
Mascots of the Guards: Irish Wolfhounds,
Frank and Doran, at Wellington Barracks,
London (1919). Their minder is Private Doyle.

Below:
Irish Guards at Warley Barracks, Essex (1919).
The group includes Valentine Castlerosse,
Tom Vesey (Colonel), Jack Broughton and
Claude Chichester (Lord Templemore).

The Feast of Corpus Christi at Warley Barracks, Essex (1919). Bishop Keating giving Benediction. This was the first Roman Catholic procession to be held in an English barracks since the Reformation.

Right:
The Commanding Officer, Lord Cavan, presenting shamrock to the Irish Guards on St Patrick's Day at Warley Barracks, Essex (1919).

Below:
Rudyard Kipling with the Irish Guards at Warley Barracks, Essex (1919). Kipling lost a son in the Irish Guards during World War I and wrote a two-volume history of the regiment.

Guardsmen parading through the streets of Windsor on their
return from the Front in December 1918.

Sergeant Moyney VC, "with Andy Duggan (my Orderly) and Bergin (my Servant)" at Warley Barracks, Essex (1919).

On the Road

Father Browne did not have a car of his own but he often managed to borrow one, preferably a high-powered one. Reports of his fast but accident-free driving are numerous. He was also driven from place to place by friends. Some of the photographs in this chapter are clearly taken from the front passenger seat. In East Anglia, Lady Ashburnham put her chauffeur, Boxall, at the priest's disposal: not all of these journeys were accident-free, as the candid camera records.

Mending the road, near Kirkby Row, Norfolk (1933). This road was subject to frequent inundations from the nearby river.

Right:
*Motor-cyclist overtaking horse-drawn traffic, Lincoln
(1934).*

Below:
*The family cow follows its owner with horse and cart
along a country road near Bungay, Suffolk (1935).*

Facing page:
*'Learner' cyclist heading towards High Street, Lowestoft,
Suffolk (1933).*

Traction-engine puffing its way up Old Street, Beccles, Suffolk (1933). An MG sports-car is overtaking.

*'A Tight Fit'
on a
Yorkshire
road near
Leeds
(1926).*

Right:
Not a flood, but a ford on the main road near Dunwich, Suffolk (1931). The passengers are heading for the marquee in the background to hear a sermon from Fr Fabian Dix OP.

Below:
Hesitating before entering the ford at Norton, Suffolk (1930).

Left:
"The most picturesque garage in England" was how the photographer described this Japanese-style extravaganza at Park Langley near Beckenham, Kent (1931).

Below:
The 'Pointsman in a Tub' at Pottergate, Lincoln (1934). The cathedral dominates the sky-line.

Right:
Driving through the Mersey Tunnel between Liverpool and Birkenhead (1935).

Below:
Lady Ashburnham's chauffeur, Boxall, having his name taken by a policeman after colliding with a tram in Norwich (1933).

On the Rails

Railways fascinated Father Browne. His Collection contains nearly two thousand photographs of railways and railwaymen, stations and passengers, locomotives and goods-wagons, dining-cars and travelling post-offices, taken throughout these islands as well as in South Africa, Australia and mainland Europe. In England he travelled mostly by LMS and LNER but he sometimes took the Great Western route to Ireland from Paddington Station to Fishguard. His pictures on the London 'tubes' repay prolonged study.

St Paul's Cathedral, London, taken from the train crossing Waterloo Bridge (1936).
An interesting photograph this, not least because many of the riverfront buildings were destroyed during World War II.

Right:
Signals at Crewe Junction (1930), the most complicated interchange in England. A train-spotter's paradise!

Below:
The Manchester to Huddersfield train (LMS) photographed between Mossley and Stalybridge, Lancashire (1947).

'On the Tube',
London (1936).

Right:
In the dining-car of the Great Western train between London and Bristol. Taken near Swindon, Wiltshire (1936).

Below:
Polishing the silverware in the dining-car of the Southampton train, Hampshire (1930).

Facing page:
A friend of Father Browne (reading one of his photographic magazines) on the London-Holyhead train near Watford Junction, Hertfordshire (1930).

'On the Tube',
London
(1936).

A little embroidery to while away the hours between London and Fishguard. Taken near Reading, Berkshire (1936).

Right:
The miniature railway at Great Yarmouth (1931) was a tourist attraction for adults as well as children.

Below:
View from the Bridge: crossing the Manchester Ship Canal on the LNER between Runcorn and Widness (1930).

On the Water

The Norfolk Broads today are full of motorized craft of all sizes and descriptions. In Father Browne's day there were just a few powered ferries across the main rivers and a single pleasure-cruiser at Breydon Water and at Oulton Broad. For the rest it was plain sailing and, of course, swimming. Modern water-sports such as wind-surfing were yet to be invented. But 'messing about' in small boats, then as now, was a particularly English avocation.

A packed cruiser going through the lock gates at Oulton Broad, Norfolk (1933).

Right:
Mersey Ferries plying between Liverpool,
Birkenhead, Wallasey and Bootle (1939).

Below:
Sailing at Oulton Broad near Lowestoft (1933).
The estuary of the River Waveney is a delightful
place that still attracts many visitors during the
summer months.

'The Pilot' working his machinery to enable the car-ferry to cross the Yare at Buckenham, Norfolk (1935).

Charles Hastings with his sons, Michael and Francis, aboard
The Copper King *on the River Waveney, East Anglia (1935).*

113

Windmill in the Norfolk Broads near Reedham (1933).

Regatta on the River Waveney, between Norfolk and Suffolk (1933).

115

Above left:
Sunset at Ullswater in the Lake District (1928).

Above right:
Reflections in the marshes near Beccles, Suffolk (1930).

By the Seaside

As a result of the mustard-gassing he suffered in April 1918 near Passchendaele in the south of Belgium, while serving as Chaplain to the Irish Guards, Father Browne had weak lungs and always enjoyed a sea breeze. The photographs in this chapter not only show fun and games by the sea but also reveal more serious interests. Coastal erosion was a menace along the east coast of England and the fishing industry (both inshore and deep-sea) was crucial to the local economy.

Lady Butler admiring the sunset at the Eddystone lighthouse, off Plymouth, Devon (1925).

Facing page:
Lighters in the Royal Albert Dock, London (1924). It was from here that Father Browne set sail, via Falmouth, for Cape Town and Melbourne.

Below:
Coastal erosion: checking the defences against the North Sea at Pakefield, Suffolk (1930). A terrace of houses in Pakefield had been lost to the sea in the 1920s.

Right:
The pilot's boat off Falmouth, Cornwall (1924). On this occasion the pilot was steering SS Port of Melbourne *just off* Pendennis Castle.

Below:
On Garton Strand (1931). The steamer on the horizon is heading for Hull.

Right:
Hugh Taylor and his model boat near
Hopton, Norfolk (1936).

Below:
Cricket on the beach near Bridlington,
Yorkshire (1931).

Right:
Fishing boat with floodlight at Covehithe, Suffolk (1933).

Below:
Punch and Judy show, complete with Union Jacks, on the strand at Walberswick, Suffolk (1933).

'Surfriders' on the North Sea coast near Turnstall, Humberside (1931).

*Facing page:
On the esplanade
at Lowestoft,
Suffolk (1933).*

*The wicket is
taking spin at
New Brighton,
Cheshire (1935).*

The lighthouse at New Brighton (1935) overlooks the mouth of the River Mersey and matches the light at Bootle.

INDEX